Women of Spirit

Insights & Inspirations
from Leading Women

vol. I of *The World Voices Collection*

edited by
Deborah A.F. Jones

A Publication of
Visions of a Better World Foundation, USA

In recognition of and as a contribution to
the United Nations Fourth World Conference on Women,
held in Beijing , China, 1995

WOMEN OF SPIRIT
Insights & Inspirations from Leading Women
vol. I in *The World Voices Collection*

Published by
Visions of a Better World Foundation, USA (VOBWF)
83 Silver Hill Road
Sudbury, Massachusetts 01776 USA

ISBN 0-9641912-2-9

Cover art and book design by Deborah A.F. Jones.
Edited by Deborah A.F. Jones, Gayatri Naraine and Rita Cleary.
This publication was typeset in Brunella.

Manufactured in China through Palace Press International, San Francisco.

*Dedicated to
the next generation of
Women of Spirit*

Acknowledgements

The editors are extremely grateful
to the following individuals for their assistance and
advice in the publication of
Women of Spirit.

Alice Andrews, Lisa Beutler, Adrienne Candy,
Denys Candy, William Cleary, Susan Dupre,
Karina Fassett, Luciana Ferraz, Janis Hashe,
Jon Jones, Lori Joyal, Karen Speerstra,
Mary Taggart, Rosmarie Uy, Maria Verrier,
Belinda Wescott, Meredith Young-Sowers

Contents

Introduction

Women of Spirit is published in recognition of and as a
contribution to the United Nations Fourth World Conference
on Women, held in Beijing, China, in September 1995. The
stories featured here emerged from interviews with women
in leadership positions around the world. "The Global
Vision Statement,"* excerpted from the book, *Visions of a
Better World*, served as a starting point for conversation.
In this context, the interviews address women's issues and
the transition from a state of oppression to empowerment.

These remarkable women tell their own stories, in their
own voices, and share personal insights with candor and
sincerity. Their storytelling teaches gently and profoundly.
Readers are given precious glimpses into the childhoods
and private places in the daily lives of these women. They
share their visions, insights and opinions on topics such as
affirmative action, community, God, karma, role models,
tolerance, world peace and volunteerism.

Discussion of spirituality is as diverse as it is omnipresent
in their stories. These eight women have very different
personal histories and spiritual backgrounds. No attempt
was made by the editors to homogenize their positions. The

acknowledgment and respect of diversity is prerequisite to exploring the universal truths of the human condition.

Women of Spirit is the first book in *The World Voices Collection*, a series of annual publications which collect and present voices of wisdom and insight from around the world. The Visions of a Better World Foundation, USA (see Appendix II) has made this work possible and will strive to continue the conversation started here.

---

* The Global Visions Statement appears in Appendix I and was excerpted from the book, *Visions of a Better World.*

Editor's Note

In my vision of a better world, people speak the truth with ease and free will. In a better world, people are empowered by the truth and know they have access to it always. I have seen a glimpse of that vision in the last six months as I have talked with these women of spirit, who have discovered their own truth and, in doing so, have tapped the source of absolute truth that connects all things.

Interviewing these women was a profound and spiritual experience, which elicited my own awakening. I am astounded by the depth of the relationships formed in one-hour conversations. These are extraordinary women, who touched my soul and opened me. I am grateful to have met them, and it is an honor to be entrusted with the custody of their words.

I regret not having the opportunity to meet Janet Jagan, and I would like to thank Gayatri Naraine for interviewing her in Guyana.

-Deborah A.F. Jones

Forward

I will not die an unlived life.

I will not live in fear

of falling or catching fire.

I choose to inhabit my days,

to allow my living to open me,

to make me less afraid,

more accessible,

to loosen my heart

until it becomes a wing,

a torch, a promise.

I choose to risk my significance;

to live

so that which came to me as seed

goes to the next as blossom

and that which came

to me as blossom,

goes on as fruit.

Dawna Markova, Ph.D.

Pregaluxmi Govender

Pregaluxmi Govender is an African National Congress Member of Parliament in South Africa and a women's and community activist. She was the Project Manager for the South African Women's National Coalition. As a Trade Unionist, Ms. Govender helped to establish the first worker's college in South Africa for developing trade union leadership. She has a daughter and a son and currently resides in Cape Town, South Africa.

Vision

I have a vision of a society in which all individuals have the ability and the basis to develop to the best of their potential. There is this feeling that sustains me: there is a goodness of the human spirit. I would like women to love and respect themselves and each other, and to have the courage to be creative and to take control of their lives.

Power

Part of my education work in the unions and in women's organizations was rebuilding a sense of community. The first challenge was to get people to have confidence again, to sense their own power, and to understand their own power. When people discover their own power, they discover love and respect for themselves, and for each other. This gives them the ability to act as individuals, and the ability to act together to change things. The second challenge was to redefine leadership, which is about following as well as leading. When a real leader's work is done, the people will say, "We've done it ourselves."

We must also redefine power. In South Africa, power has operated in terms of race, class and gender hierarchies. The terms underlying power have been competitiveness, exclusion, fear, and so forth. Really changing things is not only about accessing power as it exists. We have to redefine and transform the very nature of power itself.

The Politics of Spirituality

Knowledge and truth should not be owned or colonized. For example, the basic truths of Hinduism are not dogma;

they are not religion in that sense. A basic concept of Hinduism is that any path to the truth is valid. Therefore, a deep respect for all philosophies is inherent in Hinduism. These concepts and truths are part of an ancient knowledge, which belonged to the people of India who were colonized during the Aryan invasion of India centuries ago. The colonizers became the upper caste, the rulers of that society. The current interpretation of Hinduism focuses on the social practices which keep rulers in power. The ancient knowledge now rests in the hands of a small number of people, but rightfully belongs to all of the people of India. Knowledge is power. It often becomes colonized, but in fact, knowledge is the inheritance of the world.

When actions are motivated by religious and spiritual people, there is a tendency to keep the spiritual area unquestioned, as if it is separate from the reality of politics, control issues and organizational and power hierarchies. Yet, people often use religion and spirituality to a political end. Just as the world of politics has to be challenged around the value systems with which it operates, religious and spiritual organizations have to challenge themselves. It is inevitable; the reality of politics appears in all organizations. If we don't examine political, economic and historical realities, we talk about spirituality in a vacuum.

Diversity

Change needs to happen at so many levels: at an economic level, at a political level, at a social level and at a personal level. It has to happen in many places at the same time. On an individual level, there are many places for women to begin, and different situations require different responses. It is important not to see women as a homogenous group. There are very important differences that do exist.

It is dangerous to ignore our diversity. A good example is the issue of affirmative action in South Africa. When gender issues are examined alone, while ignoring the issues of race and class differences, the result of affirmative action is that middle-class, white women are promoted into positions and black women are excluded.

Empowerment

Breaking the invisibility and the silence of women is very important. We must make sure that the voices of the least empowered are heard. Recently, I was at a workshop attended by many people from foreign countries. The entire workshop was dominated by the foreigners, who were obviously wealthy, powerful individuals. They had very good intentions, but they did not allow the people from South Africa to be heard.   A very important and often overlooked component of empowerment is listening. We must listen very closely to what people have to say, because empowerment does not come from outside. Governments cannot do the empowering; they can only facilitate it through the redistribution of resources. We cannot empower someone else. It is a process that people engage in by finding and recognizing their own power.

Empowerment is being able to act to change things. It is not only about anger at injustice and suffering. It is not only about having a deep feeling of love. It is about combining these to have the courage to act as effectively as possible. I stress the importance of people acting to take control of their lives. Action is critical. When I do something, I learn what it is that I can do. Alone and in community with other people, I learn my power and I see my power in action. I learn that I can take control of my life at a political level, an economic level, a social level, and a personal level.

There is a resolve that permeates South African society.
Amidst all the dreadful suffering, the people are often
sustained by their own sense of humor and optimism, and
the vision and determination to act to change their lives.
When I was a trade unionist, one of the issues we dealt
with was strip searching. Management in the factories
randomly subjected women to what would effectively be
an internal examination, but by a security guard, not a
doctor. It was horrific. We held a meeting, and we asked
women to say how they felt. We asked what they thought
needed to be done. One by one, women stood on the
canteen table and talked about what they felt. They cried,
and there were women who were angry. The result was a
determination that they would not allow it to continue. The
women took action in a clothing factory. When the time
came to be strip searched, they refused to go, and demanded
management come to the floor. Then they started to take their
clothes off and showed their bodies. Management turned
and fled. The women laughed – it was hilarious! The practice
ended – they had won!

Linkages

The struggles to transform human relationships are the
most difficult and they are at the core of the transformation

of the world. The struggle to change ourselves, the struggle to change our relationships and the struggle to change the world seem to be exclusive of each other, yet they go hand in hand. What scares me is when people retreat into themselves. The development of the self is an absolutely essential component of involvement in the development of other people.

There is danger in neutrality. We cannot afford complacency or apathy. Women's issues must be viewed in context, within the complexities of the larger issue of oppression. We must address women's issues within the matrix of class, race, caste, age, disability, sexual orientation, marital status, and the list goes on. We cannot be blind to any other form of oppression. During the period of Nazi Germany, Martin Niemoeller wrote, "In Germany, they came first for the communists, and I didn't speak up because I wasn't a communist. Then they came for the Jews, and I didn't speak up because I wasn't a Jew. Then they came for the trade unionists, and I didn't speak up because I wasn't a trade unionist. Then they came for the Catholics, and I didn't speak up because I was a Protestant. Then they came for me, and by that time there was no one left to speak up." We cannot be blind to any other form of suffering. Open your eyes to the linkages. If you think you are fighting against oppression only for yourself, you are not.

We cannot talk about spirituality without talking about human reality and concrete changes. There must be concrete delivery of health, housing, jobs and clean water. There must be an end to violence against women. There must be human rights and there must be equality. There must be an educational system that nurtures intelligence and creativity and enthusiasm. There must be concrete changes that enable the development of the soul.

Kaoru Nakamaru

Kaoru Nakamaru is Chairperson of The International Affairs Institute for World Peace and Founder of the Following the Sun Association. As an interviewer and the producer of a documentary television series aired in Japan and the United States, Mrs. Nakamaru has met with hundreds of world leaders. She is married with a son and daughter and resides in Tokyo, Japan.

Personal Diplomacy

As a young woman, I thought a great deal about world peace, and I knew that happiness and peace only come from within. When people look outside themselves for power, money or fame, it is very difficult to obtain happiness inside. I wanted to talk about these ideas and so I thought I should meet with the world's leaders, kings, presidents, and famous world figures. In 1970, my goal of "personal diplomacy" led to the idea of a television series, which eventually was shown throughout Japan and on PBS in America. By 1976 I had met almost two-hundred world leaders.

The Master of the Self

On March 11, 1976, I had a fantastic spiritual experience. I realized that life is eternal and reincarnation is true. We have a great resource within us: the accumulation of knowledge and experience through reincarnation over many lifetimes. Once we realize this, with meditation, prayer or some way to connect with that resource, we can become the master of the self.

Once I realized that life is eternal, I concentrated on cleansing my soul to be able to receive the wisdom and vibration of the higher powers. It is just like cleaning a big room. You begin by taking away the big pieces of trash and dirty things; then you clean all the small things. In the same way, I did that in my soul. My conscience connected with God and I looked at myself as a third person. Every time I have done this, I have felt fantastic lightness. I see dark smoke going out and sunshine coming into my heart.

Harmony and Heart

The only thing we carry to the next world is the soul, not a big house or power or fame. I believe the first purpose of life is to have a harmonious heart. The second purpose of life is for people to work together to create a better world, a more harmonious world, and a world of peace. There are only these two purposes; everything else is the method to achieve them. For example, being a woman, a teacher, a camera-man, a journalist or a prime minister are simply methods to achieve the two purposes of life.

The world we live in is the third dimension and the spiritual world is the fourth dimension. We are all connected with the spiritual world and at least five other souls while we are here in this world. These souls are like sisters and brothers, who watch us all the time and send us all kinds of vibrations. However, if our own vibrations are very rough and we have strong negative feelings inside, it is very difficult to receive these vibrations. Once we open up our souls and hearts to become harmonious, we "tune in" and are able to receive these vibrations.

We came to this world to correct our defects. We should not be afraid of hardships, but instead, see them as a chance to challenge ourselves. They are the only way to conquer spiritual weakness. If life is just a good time,

without any hardship, we would do as well to stay in heaven. We don't do any of the work in heaven. We come to this world to harbor spiritual self-achievement and to become a harmonious person with well-balanced intellectual power, emotion, instinct and reasoning.
A harmonious person has balance in these four areas.

World Peace

In the effort to achieve world peace, I focus on the way of life, rather than the way of power. When some people talk about creating world peace, they intend to achieve it through the power of governments. The world peace I am interested in is based on the human spirit. There is a big difference. When individual people begin to realize the power they have inside, their spiritual power, this is what will bring about world peace.

When people awaken, they reach the ocean of the soul, which is connected throughout all human beings. Therefore, every one person's awakening is very important to world peace. I believe that if one tenth of the people on this planet achieved peace inside, we would instantly achieve world peace. There is a theory called "The Hundredth Monkey." Scientists demonstrated that when one monkey started to wash her food in ocean water before eating it, all the other monkeys who could see her did the same thing. When the number of monkeys washing their food reached a critical mass, somehow, monkeys on other islands also started washing their food. Within the ocean of the soul, we humans are all connected. At a certain point we will reach a critical mass. World peace is not something far away.

World Leaders

Having met so many world leaders, I believe that unless there is happiness inside them, and harmony among them, there will never be world peace. Deep, deep inside, all our leaders have a conscience, a beautiful soul, but they cover it up with many layers. One of the most important things we can do is encourage our world leaders to be honest about their spirituality. They worry about this too. For example, King Hussein of Jordan has humbly asked me about my spiritual experience, and has talked to me about his own spiritual matters. It is not different for them just because they are leaders.

Spirituality and Children

Women have such an important role because of our spiritual connection with children. Giving them our love and wisdom is very important. My husband and I raised our children so that we have a very strong and loving connection. We have a twenty-seven year old son, and a twenty-three year old daughter. They have grown up to become very spiritual and they are very caring. The four of us have totally different roles and do different work, but our spiritual tie is very strong. Wherever we are in the world, we are always connected.

Once children understand the value of life, not based on materialism but from a spiritual perspective, their total outlook is different. They will not be afraid of hardship. Instead they will choose to take chances to develop and connect with the higher self.

Each of us is a child of God. We have a light inside that is the soul. Peace and happiness come from inside, from the pureness of the soul facing God.

Each woman must realize the power she has inside: her spiritual power, her wisdom and her intellectual power. She must also recognize the influence she has on the future by teaching her children. In these ways, each woman has the opportunity to work toward world peace and creating a better world.

For many a year, I've watched the women leadership to and fro,
The mighty women, the little women, the speedy and the slow;
And many a time I've told myself that someday I would go,
Around the world that is so full of wonders.

The fast and the stately women, how they run without rest,
The women, the beasts of burden,
Oh! they have all dipped and pressed,
Around the world that is so full of wonders.

The things I've heard, the things I've read,
the things I've dreamt might be,
The women's tales, the old women's yarns,
they will not pass from me,
I've heard, I've read, I've dreamt, but all the time I've longed to see,
Around the world that is so full of wonders.

So year by year, I watch the women leadership to and fro,
The famous women and the women I've learnt about.
Little folks laugh to hear me saying that someday I will go,
Around the world that is so full of wonders.

- Beverly G. Otieno
  age 14
  Nairobi, Kenya

Flerida Ruth P. Romero

Flerida Ruth P. Romero is an Associate Justice of the Supreme Court of the Philippines. Prior to that appointment, she was Special Assistant to the President of the Philippines, Corazon C. Aquino. Mrs. Romero is pictured here receiving an award for "personal achievement and dedication to the highest standards of her profession" from her Alma Mater, Indiana University School of Law. She is married with two sons and currently resides in Manila.

Responsibility

The Supreme Court of the Philippines is the highest tribunal for court decisions. The judgments rendered will inevitably affect the lives, properties, liberties or honor of the parties to the case and sometimes others who are similarly situated. As the lone woman on the Court, I am well aware of this awesome responsibility. I approach every case with a prayer that I may be an instrument of the Divine Wisdom and Love. I realize that I do not posses all knowledge, nor am I infallible, but whenever possible and wherever applicable, I use compassion and understanding.

In this regard, women can draw upon their innate intuition to grasp the truth directly. I would like to be remembered as one who tried to pursue truth and justice for everyone.

Self-appraisal

The attitude of judges springs from education in their formative years. There are some chauvinistic male judges who have not outgrown the notion that women are subordinate to men.   I think at this stage of our social and political development, women's equality with men should be recognized. These judges must transform themselves through self-appraisal.

I must effect change within me before I can effect change on other levels. This calls for objective self-appraisal, which does not flinch when negative facets of myself are revealed. One of my favorite quotes is from the book, *Thoughts for Aspirants* by N. Sri Ram, "Knowledge of the outer world has to be balanced by knowledge of self. When one delves deep into one's self, he will begin to sense there the basic identity of life and the unity of all humanity."

Sustenence

I am a child of God, His heir and joint heir with Christ.
Therefore, I partake of the essence of Divinity. I know that
there is a Power and Light within me that I should and can
call forth. I am sustained by the knowledge that I live and
move and have my being in God. I am in Him even as He
is in me. I cannot go where He is not, and therefore I am
protected by His presence from any kind of harm: physical,
psychological, or mental. I need not fear anything or
anyone. I have perfect trust and confidence in Him. He
knows all my thoughts and feelings, so I strive to keep
them pure and acceptable in His sight. I am a child of God
and so are other individuals. I salute the Divinity within
them.

I have never had well-defined ambitions. I did not have
a timetable for pursuing my aspirations. One of the things
I learned from my mother is to put everything in the hands
of God. She would always say, "Lovingly in Thy hands we
place our affairs." I never went after anything. I sought
Divine guidance in everything and, of course, wherever I
am, I try to do my best.

I have always been a student of Theosophy, the study of religious philosophy and Truth. It is grounded on the principle of universal brotherhood, regardless of gender, caste, creed, or dogma. We all have Divinity inherent in us. With God as my guiding star, I am able to treat everyone equally, with understanding and with compassion.

Family Support

The support, love and inspiration of my family have contributed greatly to who I am today. My mother was an educator, an author, a pioneer suffragette and feminist at the time when feminism was not a common word. She was a deeply spiritual lady. She taught us to show concern and to help people in need. We shared our resources with needy people, not just our money, but our time, as well as our mental and spiritual resources. My mother taught me that I must resist temptations and pressures in life. I tried to pass this lesson on to my own two sons. These are the virtues that mothers should inculcate in their children. We can teach by precept and example. Being and acting are more powerful than words.

My father died early in life. He was a lawyer, and I followed in his footsteps. My father was not dazzled by material wealth. His clients were the poor and the peasant-farmers in rural areas, who could not afford to hire city lawyers. It did not matter that we were not wealthy. He placed great value on integrity and high moral standards.

My husband is also a lawyer. Our family is composed of all lawyers. I don't know whether that's good or bad! My husband has always been very supportive of me, and often he believes in me more than I believe in myself. When I waver or am doubtful of my ability to accomplish something, he will repeatedly affirm his belief in my capacity to attain success. Beyond inspiring and encouraging me, he will put all of his resources at my command so that I dare not fail, for I cannot disappoint him. My two sons take after their father and are equally supportive of me. Throughout my career they have stood solidly behind me, infusing me with their confidence in my abilities, and boosting my self-esteem.

Reflected Glory

I admire the pioneer women achievers of our society who have crashed the sex barriers in different professions.

I salute women who can blend most felicitously the roles of wife, mother and bread-winner, and who have discharged their duties efficiently and with good humor.

All women have the power to effect change in their lives, in their communities and as their sphere of influence expands, in the world. More and more, the women of the Philippines are coming into power. They are finding their niches. In our last senatorial elections, a woman topped the election! All the women in the Philippines bask in the reflected glory of the women who succeed.

Janet Jagan

Janet Jagan (at left) is the First Lady of Guyana, wife of President Cheddi Jagan. She has one son and one daughter. Mrs. Jagan is the Chairperson of the National Commission for the Survival, Protection and Development of Children and is seen here with Ms. Daniele Brady, resident Project Officer of UNICEF.

Leadership

As a leader, you must meet with people on a daily basis and try to solve the problems that concern the community. Without that experience, leaders cannot address the long-term sustainability of the world. When you talk with people who have immense problems in their homes and in their communities, it prepares you and enables you to see the larger problems. First you look up close at people's problems, then you turn your telescope lens around and see the problems of the whole world.

When you look you will see that people around the world are fighting among themselves and killing each other. In the end, one group bears much of the burden: children. Our children bear the burden of war and poverty. It becomes clear that the poverty of the world is linked with what people in all countries do to one another. We must look at the totality of the world, seek a better condition of life for all people and eliminate the factors which make life more difficult.

Opportunity

In the early stage of our campaign for independence and the end of colonial rule in Guyana, we had to mobilize people. We found that women responded better than men, so we began to work among the women and looked deeper into their various problems. To a great extent, we were educating women about their role in society. We urged women to give their girl children opportunities for education. I would say we succeeded greatly in that, because now our girls are completing primary and secondary school and many of them are going to universities and technical schools.

The fight for women's equal rights began with the demand for the right to vote so that women wouldn't be excluded from the franchise. In Guyana, the focus is not on "feminist" aspects as seen in some countries, but more on issues such as women being paid properly for the work they do; provision for good health care, maternity and child care; pure water supplies; electricity and other amenities of life. They must have access to education, and opportunities for advancement. Women must participate in the government of the country, in the Parliament and in all aspects of life. I feel that women must give something to their communities and to the world at large. They must address the problems of poverty and war, the need for peace, and the need to raise the standard of living in their own communities and countries and every place in the world.

Understanding and Tolerance

In the early period in Guyana, religions, with the exception of Christianity, were not respected. We fought very hard to bring the same respect to the Hindu and Muslim religions as was given to Christianity. Now the three stand equally. That was our concept of how it should be in a multi-racial, multi-religious community. Respect, understanding and tolerance are absolutely necessary.

⟨ornament⟩

The work I have been doing for the last fifty years is both political and social, and focuses on such issues as health and children's issues, civil and human rights, democracy and freedom; understanding the position of people in need is very, very important. I hope, as a person, I have understood the problems and have not had prejudices.

⟨ornament⟩

The future of the new generation in Guyana starts with education. It begins in the schools by teaching racial respect and harmony, as children of all races study together. As they grow up as friends, hopefully they will not think in terms of racial, ethnic or religious differences. They will just look at people as people. I think our young people will grow up feeling confident and able to work with their brothers and sisters of all races.

A Higher Moral Standard

The slogan of our country is "One People, One Nation." We want to achieve that, because when there is greater tolerance and harmony, the nation itself can move forward.

The process now is to regain people's dignity, self respect and a higher moral standard of what is right and wrong. It takes time to restore these things. It doesn't happen overnight. It happens through the education system and through social organizations. People have to talk about dignity and self-respect. The religious groups must agree on these subjects and remind people of the qualities of human nature that should be developed. People must be honest and they must treat their fellow human beings with respect and kindness.

I wandered lonely as a cloud
that floats on high hills,
when all at once I saw a crowd,
a host of women,
beside the lake, under the trees,
chattering and wandering in threes.

Continuous as the stars that shine
and twinkle on the milky way,
they walked in a never ending line
along the margin and gay.
Ten thousand women, I saw at a glance
tossing their heads like a dance.

- **Brenda Amondi**
  age 12
  Nairobi, Kenya

Chung Ok Lee

Chung Ok Lee is Head Minister of the Manhattan Won Buddhist Temple. She is the President of the Committee of Religious Non-Governmental Organizations at the United Nations. Venerable Lee is researching women's spirituality as part of her doctoral program at New York University. She currently resides in New York City, USA.

Wisdom

Women tend to be drawn to wisdom. Wisdom is more spiritual than knowledge, and much deeper than knowledge. You can gain knowledge from books, but wisdom dwells deep in your heart. It is an intuitive, inner direction. It is like the Buddha nature, the divine nature within. Through contemplation, reflection and meditation, we can find this wisdom. Some say knowledge is power; but to me, wisdom is the real power.

I began to meditate when I was a very young child, although I did not know it was meditation. I spent a lot of time alone, especially at the dawn and sunset. I was curious about the whole universe and how it functions. This was often when I was helping my father in the field, far from the village. As the sun rose and set, I would become quiet and become one with the changing universe. At that time in my life, I had not been formally taught how to meditate; it just came from that contemplation.

Awakening

Because of my own history and experience, I have made a vow to help women who are suffering and oppressed. It is important to awaken women to reality. First, women must be made conscious of what is going on around them, and made aware of injustice, oppression and discrimination. Then, women must have a voice and participate. There are social and economic injustices here in the United States, but if you go to the Far East or Africa, the discrimination is much worse.

Women must believe they are important and are not inferior. They must understand the vital function they have in the family. Without mothers we cannot sustain the family. Without families we cannot sustain society. The role of women is tremendous. Their contribution, their care and love are worth so much, but women have been taught to believe, "You are inferior, you are nothing, you are second class." Women need to see their potential, their unlimited capacity. By any means possible, we need to awaken women.

When I was in the tenth grade, I entered a Won Buddhist temple for the first time. A woman minister was delivering the sermon. She was standing right up front in a position of authority. Men and women lay-members sat and listened to her wisdom and her preaching. I said to myself, "Wow! This is a different world." I began to carefully observe how the women ministers functioned in the community. I vividly remember that image, that model.

Women In Power

In the history of the women's movement, we sometimes ask if where we are is our own fault. After all, women give birth to boys and raise boys; and then, the boys become men and dominate. In a sense, women contribute to that. Women raise and treat sons and daughters differently, and allow men to be more powerful, more dominant, and more creative.

Women in positions of power must treat women equally. Very often, women leaders become men and treat other women marginally, because they feel the only way they can get into those positions is to be masculine. But this is not true. A woman's way of knowing and dealing with the world is unique because of our mothering nature, and because of our experience with oppression, which makes women more resilient, sensitive to the needs of others, and cooperative.

In the Won Buddhist community, we have promoted equal opportunity between men and women for about eight decades now. Our senior women use their feminine qualities to lead. Instead of a top-down order, these women bring people together in a democratic and participatory way.

Education

We have to educate mothers about women's issues. When I was young I questioned why my mother kept silent and why she didn't challenge my father. She never complained; she just endured and my father made all the decisions. I want to ask mothers to treat boys and girls equally. Little girls may not express everything, but they observe everything. They learn who they are by observing how parents treat them as compared to how their brothers are treated.

My father tried to stop my education at the ninth grade. He believed modern education spoiled young girls. Even so, with my teacher's support, I moved to the city and continued my schooling. During that time, if I visited my family, the village people would not receive my greeting because they thought I was spoiled. They laughed at me a lot. Because of that, I developed great inner strength, and my inner direction became more clear. I thought to myself, "I cannot convince you now. But I will prove it in ten, twenty or thirty years. I will prove it later." It was a silent, inner monologue. I could not challenge my father, or my village people, but in my heart, I made a commitment. I would prove that women are worth educating.

When I became a public school teacher, the village people came to me to talk about it because teachers are very respected in Korea. Their attitude was very different. Finally, they praised me, but the process of getting there was very difficult. After twenty years, my father apologized to me in front of the whole family. He said, "I apologize, because I didn't know. At that time I did my best to protect you. That's why I tried to stop you. I didn't mean to cause you so much trouble and suffering." It was the happiest moment in my life! Now my father is proud of me and respects me as a spiritual teacher. He asks many questions about the Won Buddhist teachings and wants to learn from me. People can learn and change. I respect him for changing and becoming an enlightened father.

Change

I recently returned to Korea at the invitation of the Korean Conference of Religion and Peace. I delivered a talk on women's issues to leaders from many different religious communities. I asked them, when they went back to their homes and communities, to begin by changing themselves. Women must show respect for women in leadership positions and give them the same authority as men. I want women to be consciously aware of their own prejudice and discrimination. I asked them to treat and raise their sons and daughters equally. Many women confessed afterward that they were not aware of their own discriminating behavior. We need to start looking at women as important members of society. We have to respect them, support them and allow them to develop their full human potential.

❧❧❧❧❧

I have to begin with myself, by changing my heart and becoming awakened. Women can change their attitudes and create change in their families, villages and countries, not only by being a loud, visible force, but simply by being an example, by embodying what they perceive is a better way to be.

My vision of a better world is one in which every child born could expect to be loved by those close to her, respected by all others, to have her physical, social and intellectual needs met by her family and her society and to have no limitations placed on her pursuit of creative and spiritual fulfillment. It would be a world which will expect from her an offering of her gifts and talents toward the enrichment of her community and her world and toward an exchange of special gifts and capacities with others, within and outside her community, so that the fullness and diversity of the human family might be enjoyed and enhanced, and others perceived as a source of human richness.

- Betty Reardon, Peace Educator, USA
excerpted from
Visions of a Better World, p. 75

Barbara Hansen

Barbara Hansen worked as a U.N. Volunteer from 1993 - 1995 under the Umbrella Project to facilitate Poland's economic reform program. Mrs. Hansen pioneered and implemented the idea of a Volunteer Center in Warsaw, Poland while serving as an Advisor to the Support Office for the Movement of Self-Help Initiative. She is married with two daughters and one son and resides in New York City, USA. Mrs. Hansen (at left) is pictured with Waldemar Prasnowski, a Polish marathon runner preparing for the 1990 New York Marathon.

From the Seed

It is easier to influence legislation which will liberate women and provide equal rights than it is to develop mutual respect and understanding of both sexes. Although women often blame our miseries on men, we are the ones who raise them so it is our responsibility. Of course, environment affects and changes people's attitudes; it can help or hinder, but a mother's influence is enormous. What women can do and should do is influence their sons. Mothers must teach their sons how to respect women and girls, and teach them that women have desires and needs which should be fulfilled. When we are grown up, it is often too late to change. Everything should start from the beginnings, from the seed.

Inspiration and support should come from the family. I know this is very old-fashioned. My mother was an enormous influence on the way I am and the way I do things. She was always helping people for no apparent reason. As a school teacher, she was very involved in the community. My mother was always willing and always ready to help people, and I don't know if she realized how many lives she touched. It was really just part of her nature.

I met a friend from high school who knew my mother. This woman, who is middle-aged now, still tells me how wonderful my mother was. I am very moved that she remembers, since my mother died twenty-six years ago and at the time my friend was fifteen or sixteen years old. That made me realize just how big an influence she had.

I hope my children remember me the same way I remember my mother. When my son was twelve, he told me, "You are the most important woman in my life." Now he is twenty-one, but he is still very considerate and I hope he will continue to be that way. My daughters tell me they would like to find husbands like their brother. I'm ready to take credit for that because I have worked very hard with my children, trying to introduce sensitivity by teaching them to be aware of other people's feelings, to be tactful and not hurt people and to understand others. I emphasize, again, that it is really more important to influence sons than daughters. Women, I don't know, maybe they "get it" in their genes, but they will manage, more or less, to be aware and sensitive. Very often I see that men do not.

Belonging

When I was a child, money was not the most important thing in life. Today, society in Poland is aimed more toward materialistic things. My friends and I agree that our childhood and youth was not as bad as many would portray it. We didn't have cars, and we didn't have expensive foreign trips and so on. We had different things. As youths we had a certain feeling of belonging, and we had time to communicate and help each other. It wasn't so bad then; people had much more time to be together. Now, they can't quite find the time.

To Live in Dignity

There is a quote I have heard that says a society should be judged by the respect they show their history, which is the old people, and the love and affection or concern they show their future, which is the children. By getting involved in society's issues and affairs on a volunteer basis and showing respect for people who are weaker, older, disabled, not as privileged, or different from ourselves, and by helping those people execute their right to live in dignity, we demonstrate our level of civilization.

Volunteerism

Prior to establishing the Volunteer Center, volunteer work existed in Poland but it was not always accepted, acknowledged or appreciated. The nearest Polish word to *volunteerism* would be *praca spoleczna*, which literally translates as "social work" and carries with it a negative connotation because of the way the work was forced upon us. When I was growing up we did *praca spoleczna*, but it wasn't volunteer because you had to do it. With the political changes taking place in Poland, attitudes toward volunteer work are changing as well. It is slowly becoming fashionable. That is the path I have helped create and I hope it will continue. I am also trying to introduce a structure to the volunteer work by creating guidelines for how to recruit, how to motivate, and how to organize the work. I call it "professional volunteerism." I think it is important and needed for those who are getting help as well as those who are giving it.

Once people are involved in volunteer work, they feel good about themselves, but you have to make it attractive and show them that it is not just giving. By volunteering, we help each other. When you give something, you very often get in return much more than you gave. Besides satisfaction, you get experience in new areas and gain leadership skills. It is a way of making friends and being accepted and meeting important people. There are a lot of things which can be gained from volunteering. One nine-year-old boy told me it was a very good way to escape loneliness and to feel needed. It can also be a way of giving something back to society. When I met with the

Association of Abstinence in Poland, one former alcoholic told me that he is doing volunteer work because someone helped him at one point and he wants to help others now.

Learning

My son and I have been doing midnight runs in New York to feed the homeless people. We do it with a group of people during the night, starting at eleven in the evening and going until five or six in the morning. We provide food, drinks and clothing, but the most important part of this project is talking and listening to people. Even though New York is such a big and crowded place, very often homeless people don't have the opportunity to talk or be listened to. That is what we do. My son was very much against the idea at first, but after he did it once, he began to sign up for the midnight runs on his own without even asking me if I was going. He learned so much by being exposed to a part of society he would not otherwise have the chance to see. He learned to appreciate his good fortune and that nothing in life should be taken for granted. As if that wasn't enough, he was also able to add the experience to his list of high academic achievements and include it on his college applications.

Role Models

To introduce school children in Poland to the concept of volunteerism, I organized a competition among elementary and high school students for the best implemented volunteer project. As part of this program, I invited important and remarkable people in our society to visit the schools. Among them was a representative of the UNDP, United Nations Development Program in Poland. He told the students how he began his professional life with the Peace Corps and that he was very proud of that work. Another guest was a paraplegic man who has been in a wheelchair for the past fifteen years. Despite his disability, he is very active, enormously athletic, and he can dance in the wheelchair. He is an example of a person who, by becoming active himself, became almost independent. He is a great source of inspiration and positive thinking.

I think that young people in Poland really need role models, and this volunteer involvement, in which I believe so strongly, is a very good way of giving new meaning to their lives. By providing role models and teaching sensitivity to the needs of others and emphasizing satisfaction from volunteer work, we can influence our future by influencing children. In that small way, we contribute to creating a better world.

Joan Vitello

Joan Vitello is a Critical Care Clinical Surgical Nurse at Boston University Medical Center Hospital. She served as the 1994-95 President of the American Association of Critical Care Nurses. Ms. Vitello is married, and has a daughter and a granddaughter. She currently resides in Sudbury, Massachusetts, USA.

Freedom to Choose

I am free to choose my responses. I know, regardless of how chaotic my life might become, I have the freedom to choose how I respond to that chaos. I cannot be affected by the external; I have to be affected internally. I am in control of my thoughts, my attitudes and my actions. Understanding this is very empowering. I am the victor, not the victim. I am the ruler, not the ruled.

There was a very chaotic time at Boston University Medical Center, when we were in the midst of extensive down-sizing. Many of the nurses that I worked with were determined not to let the down-sizing affect the way we took care of patients. We believed that we could continue to make a difference. Regardless of outside events, we chose to honor the partnership between the patient, their families and ourselves. There is real power in choosing to take what you believe and putting it into action.

New Eyes

When we are on this journey in life, it is important that we look at familiar things with new eyes. Sometimes we will see things that we didn't see before. Each day, imagine seeing the world for the first time. Know what your mental models are and try to change them frequently. It can be hard to put into practice, but it is something I work on every day.

❧❧❧❧❧

I believe we all learn through intuition, in the sense that we gravitate toward certain people because there is something that attracts us to them. It is a sort of magnetism, something that comes from inside. Internally, if you know where you want to go, you will find people on your path that will help you. It is wonderful, but it only works if you are open to it. Every little conversation I have causes me to reflect upon what the meaning behind that conversation might be. I ask myself, "What am I supposed to learn from this?"

Self-reflection

We need to have the courage to take the journey back to the self. We can journey outward easily, but self-reflectiveness, self-awareness, and self-realization require courage.

⟡⟡⟡⟡

I can be brutally honest with myself. I will come down hard on myself if I feel like I'm picking up bad behavior, bad vibes, or bad karma. When I reflect on this I ask: What did I learn about myself? What do I need to improve? This is continuous learning. You have to learn first, in order to improve.

Shared Vision

When values are shared, vision can be shared. For example, in 1990, the American Association of Critical Care Nurses (AACN) collected information from nurses around the country. What we heard from our colleagues was that the health-care system was ailing; it wasn't working on behalf of patients. There was a shared value among us: The reason we went into nursing was to take care of patients and their loved ones. The frustration stemmed from the fact that the rest of the health-care system did not often value the patient as the primary focus of care. From these discussions, a shared vision of a health-care system that would be driven by the needs of patients and their loved ones was developed among the nurses at AACN. A feeling of empowerment ensues, as we work together to make our optimal contribution to patient care.

Powerful Influences

My very first role model was a business woman. When I was a child, Mary lived across the street from me and would share stories about her work life. I always respected her, because, even though she worked in a predominantly male environment, she held on to her principles. She never became a pseudo-male; she never took on the pseudo-masculine tendency of aggression. She was assertive, but not aggressive. By watching her, I learned that women could compete in a "man's world" without taking on their personalities, or their traits. I was always struck by this woman's willingness to do it differently.

I think role models are one of the most powerful influences on young people. I enjoy showing the children of my friends and family what a work-day is like for me. I have them shadow me for a day, so they see me in action. The daughter of a friend shadowed me for a day when she was thirteen. That was five years ago. She is now graduating from high school and she has decided to pursue a medical career. I was thrilled to hear about that!

My Grandmother

I had a wonderful, wonderful grandmother. She was a warm, caring person, not very educated, but she was intelligent. Her brilliance came from within. She was very wise and talented. I used to go into the garden with her and help her grow vegetables. She had the best vegetables. She talked to plants and trees and she really was connected with nature. That is why her plants grew, and why everything grew around her. She and nature shared a mutual love.

I watched my grandmother experience a lot of tragedy in her life, yet she was never overcome by it. Her husband left her almost penniless, but she always had her pride and she was never bitter. She always had more love to give. I remember at a very young age, wanting to be like my grandmother. By watching her, I learned to never let the tragedy in life affect me negatively, to never give up my love for life.

෴

I want to be a wonderful grandma! I want to be remembered by my granddaughter as someone who had special meaning for her, who helped her see that the world around her and everything in it is special, and that she is special.

I will teach my granddaughter this: Know yourself and love yourself. Know your limitations and know your strengths. Always seek ways to bring out the full potential within yourself. Know that the power is within, and be good to yourself.

Jayanti Kirplani

Jayanti Kirplani is the Director of the Brahma Kumaris World Spiritual Organization, London and is seen here leading a seminar on "change." Sister Jayanti is based at the Brahma Kumaris Global Cooperation House in London, U.K.

Revelation

When I was about six -- it goes as back as far as that -- I was sitting with my great-grandmother and she was telling me stories of princes and princesses and kings and queens. I remember so clearly, at that moment, thinking that the world she described was the world of heaven. How wonderful, how beautiful! At the age of twelve, I noticed that my mother treated me and my brother differently. It was the school holidays and we were out playing. My mother expected me to be in by a certain time so that I could help her with household chores. She did not have the same expectation of my brother, who was a bit younger than me, but I knew it didn't have anything to do with age. It had more to do with gender. Remembering that story of the prince and the princesses, I thought that if there were such a world in which everything was beautiful, then one of the things that would happen in that world would be that men and women would have the same rights. At the age of twelve I became aware of this and it became a great passion in my life.

During my teens, I saw a huge amount of discrimination on many different levels. At age eighteen, in the late 1960's, I applied for medical school. I was told that in London, in those days, only 20% of the places were reserved for women in the schools. I felt very angry. There is no other way to describe it. Soon after that, I started to study meditation and spirituality, which taught me that I am a soul, a spiritual being in a female body. As such, I have all choices open and available to me, simply depending on how I see myself. When I began to think of myself as a soul, I realized that my own values, my own esteem, my own dignity was something I had total freedom to choose and create. That led to a huge revelation: I just had to maintain the consciousness of who I truly am. No person can impose any restriction or any limitation on me if this is the view that I have of myself. From that moment on, I felt empowered to follow the dictates of my conscience. This awareness of the soul led me to total liberation, and of course, it has been an ongoing experience.

Knowledge

For me, knowledge means understanding. It means understanding myself and what is happening in my own inner world. That understanding enables me to deal with my feelings and my emotions as I try to listen to my conscience, that which guides me. This is the very first step of knowing myself.

The second aspect of knowledge is to know God and who God is. What are the qualities of God? What are the different facets of the personality of the Supreme? How does that personality interact with me? How can I come closer to that Being?

The third aspect of knowledge is the law of action and reaction, or karma. This is the give and take and the ins and outs of our thoughts, and the repercussions they have on the self and others. How do my thoughts lead to words? Are my words empowering or disempowering? Are they negative or encouraging? On a physical level, every action yields results to an equal extent. The same truth applies in the spiritual domain. Understanding the law of karma has led me to understand why I am in my current position. It answers, to a great extent, the question of my relationship with others, and what I face in terms of their responses to me and their expectations of me.

Knowledge of these three areas of self, God and karma-action have brought to me a huge amount of clarity, and therefore, power and empowerment.

I, the Soul

In the awareness of the eternal spirit of "I, the soul," I can see both the positive and the negative sides of being female. However, if I let myself think, "I am a woman, I am a female," then I am exposed to both sides. For example, a wonderful feminine quality is compassion, the quality of giving, the quality of sustaining, of love. The negative aspect of this feminine quality seems to be possessiveness, attachment, and the need for security on an external level. The more I was able to maintain spirituality in my consciousness, the more refined the positive side became. So the qualities of generosity, love, giving, sharing, and compassion were enhanced and made more divine. It became easy to let go of the other side: the possessiveness and the negativity. I was also able to integrate the positive masculine aspect of discernment, making decisions and having the power to implement those decisions. So in a very, very powerful way, this knowledge of the soul has not been theory at all. Application of the knowledge has been of immediate practical benefit.

Sharing Knowledge

Women need to come together to talk and share knowledge about subjects such as empowerment and leadership. Whether it's a little coffee group that gets together once a week, or a group that meets every day or once a month, or an event that happens once every ten years like the United Nations Women's Conference, we can share our awareness with every other individual with whom we come into contact. The way I think and speak and behave may seem to be a very little step, but if you consider that each one of us comes in contact with at least one hundred people in a lifetime, it has an impact on at least one hundred people. Whenever there are gatherings, I will share my own commitments and understanding, and it will happen in a very natural way, because that is what I sincerely believe.

CRCR⌒Y⌒

A few years ago, we were driving around in the central part of India and I saw color televisions in the little huts in the shanty towns! These people do not go out and buy newspapers and magazines. They don't have to; news is beamed right into their little huts. They can't escape it. I believe the media has tremendous potential, not only to entertain, but also to inform and educate. The information explosion that is part of our global society has an influence that is unsurpassed. Within the space of moments you are aware of anything that happens, anywhere in the world. As women who have positions of power and influence within the media become aware of the need to have dissemination of positive ideas, they will reach out in that way. I think this will cause a giant leap forward.

CRCR⌒Y⌒

There is another unseen force at work in the effort to distribute and share knowledge. From a spiritual perspective, it is said that when a student is ready a teacher appears. I do not mean somebody in a flowing saffron gown! The teacher may be in the form of a book or a television program, or the teacher may be my next door neighbor who has discovered some wonderful thing that she wants to share with me. If I am an individual who is searching, then my search will definitely bring fulfillment and I will come to a point where I have access to knowledge.

Community

Even though I had that initial transforming experience of knowing I am the eternal soul, if I were alone, it would have been very, very difficult to maintain that understanding. In the Brahma Kumaris community, I live with the example and the leadership of women older than myself, in whom I see the reality of what we talk about. Living in community with them has made it easy for me to gain inspiration and have affirmation that these things are real and not just theories.

As I moved along on the spiritual journey, I became aware of all the dark patches that I carry within my own being. It's like when you clean a window. At first you don't notice how grubby it has become. Then you start cleaning and you can see how mucky it is! Therefore, it requires more energy to do the cleaning properly. In those periods I often thought, "Oh this is impossible, this is really too strong, too heavy, too dark, I'm not going to be able to deal with it. Let me just give up and sit down and cry." It was the nurture and support from the community that encouraged me. They joked with me and laughed with me and jolted me out of that and said, "Go on, we believe in you, you can make it." The encouragement and the humor were wonderful and pulled me out of the moments of despair.

Without community, I would not have learned so much about myself, and I would not have had the opportunity to bring about change. Community means that I have to change, I cannot hang on to my weaknesses. I have to do something about them. If I had been alone, I would have locked myself into certain habits and mindsets and attitudes and it would have taken a lot to budge me out of that. But in a community there is no way you can hang on to the boxes and compartments. It's not possible.

For me, living and working in community has been a very specific training in being able to recognize the special attributes, talents and skills of each individual, learning to respond only to their specialties, so harmony prevails. It allows the possibility to work in cooperation and achieve results that would be impossible to attain by individuals working in isolation. By seeing each other's specialties and using only those aspects, mountains can be moved.

The Role of Women

I believe women around the world are beginning to see themselves as a global community. For example, I live and work with women from many different nations and religious backgrounds. What we find is that we simply have to see the specialties of each other, appreciate the goodness of each other. In that awareness, with that vision, we can enhance each other's goodness and it multiplies and we flow forward.

The next millennium is going to be the millennium of truth and love. I see this as being the true essence of the future, a world that is filled with total truth and total love. I see that the role of a woman, whether as a daughter or a mother or a teacher or a friend, is to usher in the new era of truth and love. A child learns so much in a subliminal way from the mother and the mother sets the whole atmosphere, the ethos of the home and of the household. It is the mother who looks far into the future to see what the spirit has to carry forward into the future and she nurtures that. At a time when the world is very, very dark, women will usher in a world of light that is filled with truth and love.

Appendix I

THE GLOBAL VISION STATEMENT

1. All people celebrate the joy of life.

2. Human rights are respected and upheld and the dignity and integrity of all people is assured.

3. People live in ways that preserve nature's ecological balance in an environment that is beautiful and clean.

4. The planet's natural and abundant resources are shared equitably and the basic human needs of all people are provided for.

5. All people have equal opportunities to realize their potential through an educational process that has human, moral and spiritual values at its heart.

6. Life within the immediate family is loving, caring and fulfilling and is the foundation for harmony within the broader human family.

7. There is respect, understanding and tolerance in all human relations.

8. People communicate openly and in a spirit of equality and goodwill.

9. Social, economic and political justice is ensured through honesty, responsibility and respect for the rule of law.

10. Governments, as representatives of their people, are committed to their well-being. People participate cooperatively in efforts for a secure and peaceful world.

11. Science serves humanity and appropriate technology is applied to ensure sustainable development and enhance the quality of life.

12. All people enjoy freedom of expression, movement and belief while respecting the liberties and rights of others.

The Global Vision Statement is a synthesis of the hopes and aspirations of hundreds of thousands of individuals from all over the world and now stands as a testimony of what a better world means to people in over 120 countries. Numbered for ease of reference only, and not to indicate any particular order of priority, each point of the Statement is featured in the book, *Visions of a Better World,* with samples of the international array of visions from which it was derived.

Appendix II

A NOTE ON THE PUBLISHER

Beginnings

In September 1993, a Global Dialogue was hosted at the United Nations by the Permanent Mission of Benin (West Africa). The event was coordinated by the Brahma Kumaris World Spiritual University, a non-governmental organization in consultative status with the United Nations and The Learning Circle, a USA-based organization dedicated to the development of learning communities. The Global Dialogue attracted leaders from many countries and all sectors of society to celebrate the launch of the book, *Visions of A Better World*, and to consider the implications and future of this work.

During the Global Dialogue, participants proposed that new national initiatives be created to continue the process of creating shared visions of a better world. In January 1994, representatives from the United States who attended the Global Dialogue responded to this call and formed the Visions of a Better World Foundation, USA.

Our Purpose

The Visions of A Better World Foundation, USA was established to "ignite the spirit" of all people to conceive and make real their aspirations for a better world.

Our Vision

People from around the world call our attention to the real possibilities of positive change at personal, organizational and community levels. One Foundation goal is to make visible the possibilities already existing in the spirit and will of the people to create a better world. The Visions of a Better World Foundation provides a framework where the women, men, and children who dare to dream and who have the courage to live by their commitment can realize their vision of a better world. By igniting the spirit of leadership and learning within all people, the sphere of positive influence on our common future expands. Together we will create a better world.

In cooperation with other national, professional and grass roots organizations, the Foundation seeks to:
  Support dialogues, celebrations and educational programs that expand awareness of and inspire people to create and live their personal and collective

visions of a better world.

- Create leverage and synergy by linking people and organizations who are committed to influencing positive change at local, national and global levels.
- Develop and implement research programs that generate collaborative processes, learning and citizen involvement for the common purpose of creating a better world.

Who We Are

The Visions of a Better World Foundation, USA is a collaborative of people committed to using their skills and resources to recreate a better nation and world. Every individual involved in this effort deeply believes that we can foster fundamental change at individual, organizational and societal levels. Our aim is to engage all segments of society: business, science, education, health-care, government and community. All religions and ethnic segments, and younger and older members of society are needed to spark the flame for humanity to create positive change together.

Appendix III

FIND YOUR VOICE

Questions posed during interviews for this book prompted an examination of the internal qualities which usher women into positions of leadership and sustain them throughout their journey.

You are invited to answer the same questions yourself, or ask them of someone you admire. The Visions of a Better World Foundation has offered to collect submitted responses and continue the conversation set forth in this book.

Send your responses to:
Visions of a Better World Foundation
83 Silver Hill Road
Sudbury, Massachusetts 01776
USA

Can you identify the force within yourself that has
sustained you throughout your journey?

How would you define knowledge? How has this
knowledge guided you and enriched your life?

What experiences in your own family life contributed to
the strong woman you are today?

Who were your role models?

What is the value of community?

How does the Global Vision Statement (Appendix I)
inspire you and elicit your support?

How can individuals facilitate the empowerment of the
next generation of women?

What does it mean to be a woman at the brink of the
twenty-first century?

To obtain additional copies of *Women of Spirit*, contact
Visions of a Better World Foundation, USA
83 Silver Hill Road
Sudbury, Massachusetts 01776 USA
tel: 508-440-9344
fax: 508-443-0887

About the Editor

Deborah A.F. Jones is an independent communications specialist and graphic artist. She received a Bachelor of Science degree in communications from Boston University in 1988. She is the co-founder of Global Visions, a membership network established to support the work of the Visions of a Better World Foundation. Mrs. Jones and her husband Jon currently reside on a rural homestead in Cleburne, Texas, USA.